Miracle Baby

Anointed by God, in My Mother's Womb

AUTHOR

Rev. Jean L. Gatewood-Harding

authorHOUSE®

AuthorHouse™
1663 Liberty Drive
Bloomington, IN 47403
www.authorhouse.com
Phone: 1 (800) 839-8640

Published by AuthorHouse 09/22/2016

ISBN: 978-1-5246-3972-3 (sc)
ISBN: 978-1-5246-3971-6 (e)

Library of Congress Control Number: 2016915307

Print information available on the last page.

DICKSON HOLY BIBLE--New Analytical Indexed Edition, Dictionary and Concordance--Authorized King James Version-1947

Scripture quotations marked KJV are from the Holy Bible, King James Version (Authorized Version). First published in 1611. Quoted from the KJV Classic Reference Bible, Copyright © 1983 by The Zondervan Corporation.

Dedication

In Remembrance of Mom and Dad, my parents, "The late Rev. Damon Jones Sr." and the late Missionary, First Lady, Willie Ann Jones. Their love for God, each other, their children, and all of God's people, left a great, great, great Legacy. They shall never be forgotten. They went home to Glory in 1970 and 1972, only seventeen months apart. To God be the Glory for such wonderful and loving parents.

Deuteronomy 6:5-7
Philippians 2:4
Matthew 7:12
John 3:16
Dedication also to a: Special Angel named, "Hollywood"

Acknowledgement

Thanks to my husband for his devotion and patience, and time. For the help he gave in servicing my computer etc., thanks Wayman.

To my nephew Ky, for his electronic skills, patience, time, and know how. I would not have completed on time, thanks Ky.

I cannot leave my beautiful niece, wife to Ky, for her being there to fill in where ever she was needed, thanks Sharla.

Thanks to God for giving me the mind set to write. Even though it took me quiet some years, He gave me the mind to stay focus. Thank you God,To God be the Glory.

Jeremiah 1:5 reads: "Before I formed you in the womb I knew you."

Psalms 139:13-16 reads: "For you formed my inward parts; you knitted me together in my mother's womb. I praise you, for I am fearfully and wonderfully made. Wonderful are your works; my soul knows it very well. My frame was not hidden from you, when I was being made in secret, intricately woven in the depths of the earth. Your eyes saw my unformed substance; in your book were written, every one of them, the days that were formed for me, when as yet there was none of them."

Job 33:4 reads: "The spirit of God has made me, and the breath of the almighty gives me life."

This is a very quiet and peaceful morning. The sun is up and the Son of God is in the room, birds are singing, winds blowing calmly and the temperature is a perfect 75 degrees. My favorite times of year are Spring and Fall. It is usually between 60-75 degrees, not too hot nor too cold, perfect for me. I serve a perfect God, who created me in His own image and spoke to my heart, saying "Jean, before you were born

I knew you". It's amazing to hear God's voice. He said in John 10:27, "my sheep hear my voice, I know them, and they follow me".

Looking back over my life, there are so many things I wish I could change. Then again I don't really know if I would want to change everything. You say double talk; not really. If I changed some things, I would truly miss, I believe, the lessons learned, the experiences, and the many blessings I received by doing what God said instead of man. In my 70 some years of living, I've had many trials and tribulations but I made it through it all by the grace of God. I've heard that saying many times, but God has let me live long enough to witness that it is a reality.

By nature, I wasn't supposed to be here, but because of God's divine intervention I am alive and well.

I am the fourth child, and the third daughter. My brother was the first born with two sisters following him. Three years later when mother thought she was finished bearing children, here I come. My dad wanted a big family, but mother only wanted three children, which was the perfect number for her. I was not born yet, but my parents and close neighbors filled me in on my miracle birth.

One morning, my brother, who collected bottles to earn a little cash, went about his usual routine. He would put the bottles in his little red wagon as he usually did and carry them to the grocery store. The day was a regular day until neighbors started to scream and howl. Every neighbor on the street was out of their house. They said as my brother was approaching the hill that led him to the store, a car came down the hill out of control and hit my brother and his wagon. When things settled, my brother was bleeding profusely. They could not take the chance of waiting to see if an ambulance was going to come in time so the men put Daddy and my brother in their car and rushed him to the hospital. They didn't have time to tell or wait on mother. While this was going on, mother was in the house cooking. She heard the confusion and went to the front porch to see what was going, not thinking it involved her family. When she opened the door and stepped out on the porch, some neighbors met her there and told her what had happened. My mother was thinking, this is my only boy, my first born, please God don't take him away from us. She was so hurt, afraid and just plain out of it that for the moment she totally forgot she was pregnant. Instead of going down the stairs, she saw the car leaving without her and she leaped off the front porch and starting running after the car. They had to run and catch her, they knew she wasn't thinking straight. They had to restrain her to remind her of her pregnancy. She passed out from so much excitement. In her right mind she would have never done what she did. They carried her back to the house and called the doctor. She said to me, she thought her world had been tossed upside down. Dad returned home with my brother and oh what a reunion that was. My mother could now relax and focus on taking care of me and her body. My brother was alive and well. He was quiet frightened and roughed up. His lip was split open and he had a cut across his eye brow. The doctors did a good job at sewing up his cuts. The cuts didn't disfigure him, but the scars were there for life.

When telling me about it years later she had tears in her eyes. Not only was she terrified of losing her son, she now had the gilt of jeopardizing her new baby, me. As mother talked I felt her pain, not knowing that years later I would be in her shoes, only with a different ending.

Mother saw me tearing up and she said, "They didn't think you were going to make it, but I prayed". Whenever Mother prayed, God heard her and answered her prayers. Mother was three to four months pregnant and nobody expected me to survive that leap and all the excitement that took place afterwards. Mother was on bed rest with the doctor monitoring her and my Dad taking charge of the house and my siblings. The doctor thought that if I survived the trauma, I wouldn't go full term. Well not only did I survive; I went full term, much to everyone's amazement. The doctor had to admit, there was a divine intervention which was unheard of. When I was born March 20th 1938, there was a great celebration in our home, praising and giving thanks to God for the "Miracle Baby", me. Mom and Dad named me Jean because I was a gift from God. My middle name came from my Auntie Louise because of her sweet, humble spirit. They wanted her name to live on through me. I love my name; I have always loved my name. My parents, knowing that it was a Miracle from God that I was alive wanted to say thank you in this manner. You see, when I looked up my name on the internet, the Urban dictionary said the name Jean means God is gracious, and He is. It further said that my name means one that is fun, sympathetic and charming, witty, brilliant and an excellent friend. Jean is the French name of Jehan. Now you may think that I'm too wrapped up in myself, and that's okay. You see, when I hear from my parents and others that it was only by God's grace that I'm here and I didn't lose my mother in the fall, I can't help but to get overwhelmed. I love God, my parents that gave me my name, my family and friends, I love everybody. I owe my life to God and I live daily giving Him the Glory.

After hearing about my traumatic experience, I wondered if I as a baby could feel the trauma, or hear the screaming and hollering. You know, they say babies can hear you talking to them. That's why parents talk to their unborn babies. I wonder what kind of experience I was going through, or if I just slept through it all. I don't recall anything, and maybe that's a good thing (smile).

But think about this, maybe there is something about babies hearing you talk to them. Thinking back on what Mother told me, she wanted only three children. That was her ideal family, but it didn't happen that way. My Dad wanted a large family, so he was happy. I tried to imagine me being in Mother's womb all warm and peaceful until one day my world was interrupted. I was being tossed to and fro, up and down in my warm home. Then things began to settle down and I could hear voices. I knew not what they were saying, but people were upset, including me, and it didn't look good for me. I could hear my mother crying out to God, "Help me Father, I can't help myself." As I said when Mother prayed, God heard her and answered her prayers. Psalm 55:17 says," Evening and morning and at noon will I pray and cry aloud: and He shall hear my voice."

I was told the story of my beginnings many times, but it didn't really sink in until that day when a police car chasing after a car in the city almost killed me. As we were riding down the street after church one Sunday, a car came from a side street and cut in front of us. We hit the brakes quickly and I heard the siren of the police car to my right and looked right in the eyes of the police. They were right in my front seat door. I couldn't open it if I tried. It was nobody but God that held their car back from hitting me. I would have been dead as fast as they were going to catch this man. We were so shocked, we couldn't move for a while. The police knew they scared us, so they backed up and pulled around us and proceeded to chase the man. I have been forever grateful to God for the many times He spared my life before, but this time He spoke and I knew His voice. I have been saying for years to my family and friends that God ordained and anointed me in my Mother's womb to serve Him. I knew people perhaps said to themselves, "Yeah, really?" But I knew. This time He called my name, "Jean, before I formed you in the womb, I knew you." Excuse me right here. I've got to cut a step for the Lord! Hallelujah, to God be the Glory! If more people were sincere about serving God, they would be getting their praise on for Him.

My parents weren't the average parents in our eyes, they were super special parents. They were highly intelligent, smart, even tempered, spirit filled, loving, and long on patience. It was clear to us as children that God had invested great wisdom in these two people, our parents. At the age of three, I made my debut as a singer. Yes, at the age of three! I told you, God had a reason for saving my life. Mother was a singer from childhood and so was her mother. Mother had a keen, high, anointed voice such that when she sang, you thought you were hearing angels from heaven. Grandmother had an anointed full contralto mellow voice that would make heaven's joy bells ring. These two women should have sung at Carnegie Hall, but I don't think the U.S. was ready for these two black melodious singers in the twenties. They spiritually blessed so many of those that were privileged to hear them.

Mother had already started my two older sisters singing with her. I'm the fourth child and the third daughter. That made my oldest sister seven and Charlotte five, and yours truly, me, three. We practiced with mother as often as we could in the midst of all her other chores. She poured her love, energy, talent into us. She loved to sing and play the piano, and knew the gift of singing should be in us. She was right. We loved it and enjoyed Mother teaching us. When Mother sang and played the piano, Dad would just sit with his head laid back on the recliner looking up to heaven with tears rolling down his cheeks. When we sang with Mother in harmony it just made his day. He gave us the name, His Bouquet of Roses.

My Mother was Baptist. She and her parents belonged to St. John Missionary Baptist Church. Our Dad belong to Campbell Chapel African Methodist Episcopal (A.M.E.) Church. I'm told that it is the Oldest A.M.E. Church East of the Mississippi. We had fun going to two different churches. Mother thought that I was ready to join the group since she had taught me the songs she and my sisters had sung, plus some new ones. I was a feisty little one, and you might add a little spoiled. After all, I'm the "Miracle Baby", getting ready to debut. This Sunday was special, as Mom was debuting her third daughter. Everyone knew of my beginnings, and she was so proud. She gave the intro and pointed to us to sing.

Much to her surprise, I froze and wouldn't hit a note. All she heard was Irma with her rich, tenor voice and Charlotte with her rich, alto voice. She looked over to me and all she saw were tears running down my cheeks. Being the professional she was, she began to sing the soprano and they were a hit. When we were finished, my two sisters lead me back to our seats. Mother looked at me with a look that I knew. "Oh God, help me," I prayed. "I'm in trouble." I just knew I was going to get it. Mother had put so much work in us and I embarrassed her. I really sound good with my sisters. It's as though I was born to make the threesome. When we got home, Mom went about getting ready for dinner. She never said another word about it, neither did my sisters. They were afraid I was going to get it, and I didn't. Whew! Thank you, Jesus! Just before dinner, she took me aside alone. She said, "If you do that again I will whip you right on the spot in front of everyone, now go get ready for dinner."

When I grew older and went to school, I knew I was going to sing in the choir because that's a part of me. One day in choir practice, our director tried our voices on the scales, up and down. When he hit the high C, I hit it. Everybody turned and looked at me. The director didn't see who hit that key, his back was to me. Of course they all told on me and I shrunk. He asked me to sing the key and I do declare, as the elders would say, my voice froze just like it did at the age of three and I had to be at least in the sixth grade. This time was somewhat different. You see, whenever I sang, they would laugh and snicker at me. They said I sounded like white people, I sang white. I don't know if they had ever heard anyone with my sound or if they were just being mean. It came natural for me to sing the key, because I sang like my mother. I did not sing that key. I didn't want them to laugh at me. I decided to sing alto and very low. I sang alto the rest of my school days. My school director started a group for professional voice and I joined it. Guess what, I sang alto and never had any more problems with people laughing at my voice. I've found in life that people get jealous of people who have a gift that they desire and instead of thanking God for the person and their gift, they let envy set in. They don't know that when you're happy for others God blesses in abundance. God just might let the mantle fall on you.

I understand why my mother spoke to me in such a harassing way. I don't believe my Mother would have done what she said, but she knew she had to put enough fear in me to never again let the group down. I was the melody, the soprano that blended the tenor and alto. She knew she could carry the group, she also knew she was still giving birth to my siblings and future siblings. She taught us to sing acapella so that when we had engagements and she could not be with us, we would be prepared. In our day there were YWCA Conventions. My mother saw to us being members of the Young Women's Christian Association. Its motto and work was "eliminating racism and empowering women". This was a great outlet for young women traveling and meeting other young girls. The ages ranged from the young girls to the older women. They embraced the Jones Sisters singing group and paid our way to the conventions. We met other singing groups and made so many friends; what a fun experience.

As our lives evolved, Dad was called by God to preach. This changed our family routine. Mother left the Baptist to help and support her husband. He was now an Itinerate Elder traveling out of town. This was a great change and an interesting experience. Where we used to walk to church, now papa had to get a car because to catch a bus to his churches was too expensive and took too long. Papa found a used car. We couldn't afford a new one, too many bills and too many mouths to feed. It was a 1950's green Ford or Chevy. We called it the Green Hornet. Dad knew he would have to fix it occasionally but right then it ran. My oldest brother by this time was off to college, attending Wilberforce College in Ohio. Wilberforce is one of our A.M.E., Church College. There were a good number of us at home and we all got in that car. We had stools for my sisters and brother when we ran out of seats! But we traveled every Sunday to the various churches Dad Pastored. Mom had me to travel with Dad when she was too tired to travel during the week. I loved that because I liked to be on the go. Of course some were envious and upset because Mom chose me. You know she had the right answer. Her answer to those that complained was, "Jean will not go to sleep on her Dad. We've been watching all of you to see who would stay awake; every one of you goes to sleep but Jean. She will talk, watch and keep your Dad alert. That's what he needs." Mother said, "Furthermore, she gets her work done on time while some of you wait to the last minute to do your chores." Well, with that, you know my name was Mud! I had it rough for a while until they saw that Mother made the right choice. You know when you've been taught to love your siblings, you can't stay mad or distant too long. Love conquers all. We were not allowed to fight and if we did we had to give each other a big hug. That's no fun, so we decided that there wasn't any use fighting if we have to hug afterward. I told you we had wise parents. They were the best.

One Sunday morning, traveling to Dad's Church, a tire blew out. Dad didn't have a spare. We were half way there, and there were no filling station around. You have to realize that these rural churches were in the country, and filling stations were many miles apart. Since we were closer to Dad's Church in Greenville, IL, he decided to travel with one side of the car on the dirt and the good side on the highway. My Father was a dedicated Pastor and he was going to get to his church, however long it took. The flat tire was flapping and making noise. We children were embarrassed and hid down in the seats and the floor of the car. Mother sat up front with her husband holding her head high and proud. She stood by her man through thick and thin. Meanwhile we were still hiding. Dad drove that car all the way to Greenville right to the front of the church. When we arrived, of course by this time we were late, and yet those faithful members were waiting. One of them took Dad's car while we were in church and had the tire fixed. The people were warm, friendly, and willing to please and take care of our needs. Mother always took extra clothes in case of accidents and food to feed her family. She was the virtuous woman without a doubt. Wherever they sent Dad and Mom, the church grew. When we went to some of the churches, no one was there. They didn't come to church until the Preacher came and someone rang a bell to inform them. The larger churches were already in Sunday school when we arrived carrying on the service. One day I asked my Dad why did they move him from his Church when he's the one that built it up? His answer was very simple. He said _____ (my nickname) and smiled. "It seems that God called me to be a builder", and he smiled and said no more about that. I was very upset because when we came there was no one or just a few. Dad and Mom having a large family attracted people with children to come see. They liked what they saw and joined our church. A Preacher who preaches real well with a readymade church made up of his family, that's a great draw. Mom played and sang and we joined her, (a readymade church). We made lots of friends and even two marriages took place in our family. Two sisters found their husbands. One in Lebanon, IL and the other in Collinsville, IL. So you see, our family just got larger. This made things very good and happy for our family. Our parents taught us the Lord's Prayer and the Twenty Third Psalm as soon as we could speak clear and plain. At an early age we knew we couldn't just be bench warmers. We had to choose what we enjoyed the most and do it. Singing for all of the girls was first, and then we could pick others, if we wanted to. Seeing Mom and Dad work so freely made us love and enjoy church and the people. Our parents loved us unconditionally and yet they kept us in check. They were very strict. When we were disobedient we were chastised and that was very few times. We were not allowed to talk back and if we did, you knew you were in trouble.

Dad said something to one of my siblings and she talked back. She was standing right behind him, so he thought, but she moved. He gave her a back hand slap and I caught the blow. I was so small and frail, I hit the floor. He was shocked when he saw me on the floor and looked stunned when he didn't see my sister. The look in his eyes said it all, I knew he was sorry for hitting me. From then on I stayed clear of her and my Daddy's hand.

We were never purposely mistreated by our parents. They worked three or more jobs to take care of us and still gave us quality time. How did they do it? They pushed themselves passed their ability. They always found time to be there when we needed them. For instance, Mom sent me to the store when I was about six or seven. As I went, I had to pass the house of a large white family. Many times they would throw rocks, but when you throw back that seemed to curb the throwing. This time one of the little girls came close to the edge of the road and called me the n, word repeatedly. I had never had that said directly to me and it hurt my feelings. I ran home crying. Everyone that was at home came to my aid. Dad was in the kitchen and came running to see what had happened. When I told him, he looked straight into my eyes and said, "Look at me. If I ever hear of you crying because of what someone called you, I will spank you. You let no one intimidate you to make you feel less than who you are. You belong to your Mother and I and that means you are somebody special. Hold your head up high and embrace your heritage". I never again from that time on let anyone hurt me with their words. This is the kind of teaching we got from Mom and Dad.

Oh, did I tell you that we were a family of seventeen children? My Mother had seventeen births, unbelievable. Mom and Dad were blessed in raising thirteen of us. Four brothers died and four lived along with the nine girls. A pretty good sports team, or a singing group. While my Mother was doing all of those jobs, cleaning, cooking dinner, washing and ironing, she had to come home and do the same for our family. At the same time, she was carrying a baby in her womb. She worked outside the home during the last seven children. What a woman. She would go non-stop day in and day out. I would look at my mother and shake my head and wonder, how did she do it. She would clean us up in the evening so that we would be fresh and clean when Dad came home. This was every day. Some days when they had a little extra strength after dinner, we would walk three blocks up to Central Avenue, to the ice cream parlor. As we licked our cones, we would find ourselves back at home. By now we're ready for bed, smiles on our faces, giving thanks to God for our wonderful parents. Ring-ring, the alarm is waking us up at four thirty a.m. to go to the office to clean. Dad, Mom, my sister and I were a team. Dad would get us started by cleaning the floors and then leave us to complete the dusting, etc. He was off to the factory to work for eight hours over that hot furnace. Once we walked back home, it was time for the rich lady to come and

pick Mother up to clean for her. As for my sister and
I, we're off to school. Just another day's journey and
I'm glad about it. Do you understand how special our
parents are to us? They could have been like thousands
of couples with large families. They said often, if we
had you, and we did, we are going to take care of you.
Some of our younger siblings know nothing about
what we went through, working outside the home.
That's a good thing because each generation should
improve. I started working when I was in the seventh
grade. It was a good thing. I could help my parents
and also help myself. I've been working ever since.
My oldest sister was a Godsend for our parents. The
next oldest also contributed to the household.

On the way home from school we were jumped on
by children who hated P.K. kids. We were only two
blocks away from home. We knew they wanted to
jump us for some time. We thought we had made it.
All of a sudden they came out from nowhere yelling
slurs at us. "You think you are better than us", they
said. I was a runner and I knew if I could get an
opening, I could go for help. I said to my sister, let's
run. She was so petrified all she could do was cry. I

had gotten tough to them because this wasn't my first encounter with bullies. I knew then that it was going to be up to me to break through, and I did. As soon as I was free I started screaming, and it was loud. The scream made them scatter, but not before hitting my sister. I hated that, but I did what I had to do to save the both of us from getting beat up by haters. We were taught never hit first, but defend yourself if you can, and I did thanks to God. We had a short walk to school, but now we had to take the long way around. Things could have been worse, but we had praying Holy Ghost parents and grandparents praying for us through our school days.

Our birthdays were celebrated on the date of our birthday. You would think that Mother would make a cake for the month and everyone in that month celebrated with that cake. No, that's not how Mother did things. Everyone got their own personal birthday cake from scratch. Party, party, never a dull moment. Mother didn't have money to spend on soda for each of us so she made Kool Aid and put it in a soda bottle. One day we were out on the back porch drinking Kool Aid Mother had made for us. Our neighbor's son saw us and thought it was soda. We could drink more than one bottle of Kool Aid and it did not hurt us. Mom being the Mom she was thought that it would be cool to put the Kool Aid in a soda bottle. She had us wash them out and she filled them up. It worked. He was very spoiled, an only child that got anything he wanted. We had all flavors and that freaked him out. He wanted to do what we did and his mother bought him the real soda. He drank one bottle after the other and got sick. You had to be there to see this kid. He started wetting the bed from drinking so much soda. His daddy got angry with him for wetting the bed and whipped him, while cursing him at the same time. It was so funny, we had to laugh and feel sorry for the kid. He was an only child and didn't know what to do with himself. Anything he wanted, they met his command. We weren't rich and actually we were poor and didn't know it (smile). My parents didn't let us know about the business end until we went to work and could contribute. My father said he wanted God to help him do three things and that was; to help him to keep a good roof over his wife and children's head, keep the house good and warm, and have plenty of food, good food for them to eat. My Dad and Mom worked side jobs to make ends meet the need. Jane and I would always go with them to make sure Mom wouldn't do too much. She would watch Dad so he wouldn't overdo it. We would always help, as much as she would let us (smile). She thought she was an iron woman, the way she would go untiringly. We were a team. My brothers helped when they were old enough. My mother was a seamstress, she was taught by her mother. She made dresses, underwear, and could take an old suit or dress and alter it to make it look modern and refreshed. With a house full of girls and money short, her gift was a Godsend. She taught us to sew and made sure we took sewing in school.

She didn't worry about us learning to cook, because she and Dad were chefs. She could out cook the highest and best chef, and Dad would be right behind her. We ate well and all from scratch, you know what I mean.

In my junior year of high school, I got engaged. A year later at the age of eighteen we were married. He had joined the service before our marriage. I only had six months to go and we knew that I could finish school in the U.S. military service. We also could travel and see the world. He didn't want to wait until I graduated because he didn't think I would be there when he got out of the service. He didn't want anyone to steal me. He was only in for two years. A red flag or light should have gone off up in my head, but it didn't. I was so in love and excited. I was the first girl of nine to marry. With Dad being a Preacher and Mom by his side a missionary, you know it was going to be big and it was. A.M.E. Preachers from all over, other Ministers, Missionaries, Church people, friends and school mates. There were over four hundred people invited to our wedding. It stirred up some controversy because I wasn't the oldest. The custom was the oldest was to get married first and in this case, I wasn't the oldest. Through much discussion my parents okayed our marriage with their blessings on one condition. My father said to my fiancée, "her Mother and I have been waiting to see her walk across that stage and receive her diploma. If she goes away with you after the wedding which is in January, we would be robbed of that celebration. We want you to understand how much this means to us. We worked hard to see all of our children graduate from high school and college.

If you agree to not take her away until she graduates, we will give you our daughter's hand in marriage". I was so torn and sad because he and I had discussed me finishing school in the service.

I cried so hard because I wanted to be with my husband. How exciting it was for me to go to Germany and be with my husband. I had saved myself for my first and only husband. I wanted the man that I married to be the very first and last man to touch me. I was looking forward to our first weeks together away from everyone. This was frightening but what the heck, I'm going to be married "wow". I thought about what Daddy said. My Mother and Father were my everything. I know how hard they had worked to take care of all of us. How tired she would be after dinner to have to get up and go clean some office buildings. We had extraordinary parents, so when they asked me to graduate first and then join, him I said yes. It was painful. I had worked hard to save up for our reception. Mom and Dad paid for my gown, it was so beautiful. I had so many hugs in the reception line they tore my veil halfway off. My husband and I had two weeks together and then he was off away from me to Germany. He had no money for a hotel room, so we rented an apartment. The apartment was rented to us from an elderly lady. She was very nice to us. About nine thirty, we heard something that sounded like switches. We thought, there are no children up there are there? We went to the stairs where the trap door was and pushed it up just enough to peek. You never would believe what we saw.

This old lady had switches whipping this little old man she lived with. She was old but very strong and bossy, poor old man. We couldn't help him, nor could we call help for him. We had nowhere else to go. We were very kind to her (smile). We had no car so we walked everywhere. It was two weeks of good fun. My Mother and Father had taught us girls that our flower was to be our gift to our husband. I'm so happy I kept myself for my husband. This was the worst part; he had to leave me behind. We didn't plan for this. Now I was married and lonesome as all get out. The first week was good, he called every night. It was that way for the first few weeks, and finally I stop getting calls and letters. They came every now and then. He began to talk about his head boss was telling him that he needed to get out and have some fun. He wasn't thinking clear and it was affecting his work. Then the letter came that he was ordered to go out with women. The letters were very few and short. It was clear to me that absence doesn't make the heart grow fonder. Well, I got mad at him and I decided that two can play this game. I was mad at God for letting me down. He could have warned me that if I didn't go with him this was going to happen. I was so mad; I said I have kept myself for nothing. For the next three years I freed myself of an absentee husband and I enjoyed my life; two can play this game. Out of the four years of marriage, we were together only four weeks. The two week honeymoon and the two weeks before he was shipped off to New York, where he said he couldn't find a place for me to stay. Enough was enough. I married again, and agian, the wrong man that wasn't ready to settle down to one woman. I can't stay with a man who's not ready for one woman and so I have to move on. If God told me to be faithful, that goes for everyone. I was choked almost until death because I went to a revival and stayed too long. God spared my life, His hands have covered me all of my life. That next year, God convicted me of my sins. I was in church from a baby, but didn't want the Holy Ghost, the keeper. I thought I could keep myself. I was always getting saved from my sins, but stopping short of the Holy Ghost. One day a preacher preaching said, "Have you received the Holy Ghost, since you believe?" I was undressed from my head to my feet. It's as though God had undressed me and I simply felt naked. That Sunday morning pastor closed service and went to the door where he always stood to greet people. We were waiting for him to say the benediction and he couldn't. The Holy Ghost was all over the church. Anyone who desired him would get their healing or whatever else they wanted. I said in my mind to God "Fill me with the Holy Ghost" and a cloud surrounded me. You couldn't see it with the natural eye, but you could see it with spiritual eyes. I heard people saying holla, stomp your feet, but all I could do was wave my hands with my eyes closed. Water was running down my cheeks profusely. I felt I was in heaven. God had filled me with the Holy Ghost. My prayers were answered. That Thursday night, the Holy Ghost came through with fire and I've never been the same. About three months later as we were traveling to Decatur for my sister in Christ aunt's funeral, we were told to put seat belts on. We didn't know that we were about to narrowly miss being beheaded. A semi-tractor trailer truck pulled out onto the highway right in front of us. The young man tried to stop, but he was going too fast. We were going to a funeral and were about to be a funeral. Just before the trunk pulled out on the road, the spirit of the Lord spoke to us to be obedient to the driver about the seat belts. Our car was headed right under the truck. God spoke to the driver to hit the shoulder and he did. He couldn't hit the brakes any longer or we would have been thrown out. When he hit the shoulder, he hit it sideways and dirt flew everywhere. The doors flew open and everything in the car was thrown out. Well, that would have been us had we not been obedient to God's voice. He said He knew me before I was born, and I believe it. I wouldn't be in this world without Him. I got a strong tower in the Lord. Some people put their hope in their money, some their family and so on. But I put my hope in God. We tried to tell some friends that a while back and they didn't listen. You see when you need help, you have to go to the right source. Our friends were looking for directions to St. Paul. They were going on a trip with the kids and family. It took them all day and part of the night. We asked them, "did you call the road service for help; you know they can map that out for you? Have you got it right?" "Yes", they responded, "leave it to us guys, we're alright. You all just take care of the kids and the packing, we got this". They had bought walkie-talkies to communicate with each. We got up about five a.m., packed the cars and started out for our vacation trip. We left Peoria heading for a good time. We drove about two hours and they wanted to know if they were on the right track. One yelled at the other, hey, here comes a sign, lets, see how far we've traveled. Much to our surprise, it said "WELCOME TO PEORIA".

It's the same with life. You can travel hear for many years, going nowhere. Unless you go to the right source, you're wondering around and around just as they did in the wilderness. Jesus is your source, God said so.

We were blessed with parents that talked to us and explained things. Their story of how they met is worth repeating over and over. It was so romantic and so special. Their connection reminds me of Ruth and Boaz in the Bible. Ruth and Boaz's meeting was a divine intervention of God, the same as Mother and Dad's meeting about fifty seven years ago. My Mother found her Boaz at the well as she was getting water. His father, Grandfather Jones, had told him that the first female he saw at the well, was going to be his wife. If she wasn't of age, then he was to wait until she was. But wait now, there seems to be a story here, a real good one. When he saw Mother at the well he gently approached her. He told her the story his father had told him. You see, he believed what his father had told him. It is obvious that his father's word was trust worthy. He proceeded to tell her to go home and tell her mother what he had revealed to her. Because of her age, she was told by my then future Dad, to go home and save herself for him. Being only thirteen years old, she was frightened and excited at the same time. My Grandmother had another young man, one of her classmates in mind for her. Mother let her know that she knew, the man at the well was the only future husband she wanted. Mother was a small well shaped young lady. She had dimples, a little pug nose, beautiful brown skin, and long black curly hair. Dad said he was smitten by her at first glance. Dad was a high yellow man, as they say, a very handsome, clean cut young man, that walked with a cane and wore a black derby hat. He always wanted to be older than he was, so he raised his age a year older. Grandmother saw how overwhelmed she was and set forth to meet him and find out what his intentions were. After all her daughter was only thirteen, what is going on? My future Father repeated the prophecy concerning Mother to her and she too was overwhelmed with the prophetic prophecy. Prophecy was one of Grandmother's gifts. As they stood together, the spirit of God spoke to Grandmother and said, "He's the one". Grandmother said God knew she did not like him because of his flare, but when God spoke, that settled it. When mother turned sixteen, they were married. Papa said when he saw Mother she looked like a beautiful sweet kitten, so he nicknamed her Kitty. He called her Kitty for as long as they lived. Never once did I hear Papa call Mother by her first name, Kitty it was for life (smile). Mother had her Boaz, and Dad had his Kitty. A year later came their first born, a son name after Dad, Damon Jones Jr. Dad had no middle name. Two years later came Irma, two years later came Charlotte, and three years later came me, the "Miracle Baby". My Mother wanted only three children, she thought she was through, but "OOPS", here I come. Daddy won, he wanted more, but he got more than he bargained for. They loved every one of us and thanked God for His many blessings upon us.

As I previously said I know the pain my mother went through when she thought she had lost me. As I raised my three stepchildren, I also dreamed of giving birth to my own children. I finally got pregnant with my own child. I was so happy, and that night when I went to church, I testified to God's goodness and how he had blessed my womb to conceive. Nobody told me not to dance and shout, so I did. I gave praise to God in dance every chance I got. When I felt the baby kick, that was one of the greatest thrills in my life. But then one day, I went to the bath room in terrible pain. As I sat on the stool, blood came running from my body. I looked and saw large clots of blood. When it was all over, I ran to the phone and cried out to my mother, "What is going on?" I told her of my experience, and she said, "Jean, you've just had a miscarriage." I cried for days, blaming God for my loss. "Why, why, did you let this happen to me? You know how much I love children, and have waited for this. I serve you, I love you, I live for you, why? Women that don't want children are having children. I want children and you let mine die, why?" He never answered me. I lost it. I refused to stop wearing my maternity clothes for months. I was totally lost in myself. My family and church members never said a word; they just continued to pray that God would bring me out of whatever I was going through. I was told that I could never get pregnant again, that's when I thought about suicide. I knew then that I needed God to reverse my thinking. I went on a long fast, asking God to restore my faith, and renew His spirit in me. He said to me, "First come out of those clothes." Once I took the maternity clothes off, reality set in. I cried until I couldn't cry anymore. My stepchildren would come and pray for me. You see I taught them about God and His Son Jesus. They knew about the Holy Ghost, because they were there when I was filled along with the Pastor, and others. That was a joyful day. As my stepchildren prayed for me, God began to speak. He said "look around and see how I have blessed you with children that love you dearly. You've proven to be a good mother and they have profited because of you. There is a reason why and you will find out by and by."

I was born in a nice sized family that got bigger, and bigger. There was never a dull moment, and there was lots of love and fun to share with each other. Mother and Dad were wise parents who let God lead them as how to manage all of us children. That all of us would know their love was real and equally spread out to each of us. We knew and felt just how much they loved us by how much they sacrificed for us. I simply can't explain how dedicated they were to God, to us, and the many parishioners they cared for and shepherded.

Daddy Damon

Whenever we went out, Mother would remind us to mind our manners, watch our conduct, and our attitude. She said our actions reflect their training, so to be on our best behavior at all times. As the girls grew older, we were finally the nine Jones Sisters Ensemble and Co. We sang with the James Cleveland Workshop of America. We traveled from city to city singing in concerts of our own and concerts with other groups. We sang with the S.I.U. Community Concert Choir, under the directorship of Dr. Hedly. He also directed us in concert with the St. Louis Symphony Orchestra. We sang as the Jones Sisters Ensemble at the Kiel Opera House in a Gospel Fest. We sang on the Charlotte Petterson Show live on television, and the list goes on. I've been a professional singer for years, doing concerts throughout Chicago, Decatur, Peoria, Iowa, Memphis, Detroit, and many other cities. Singing is one of my gifts from God.

The *Jones Sisters Ensemble*
of Alton, Illinois

When I lived in Chicago, I met a Mary Kay Director at the house of one of my friends. She invited me to try the skin care and then the makeup. I was so impressed and pleased with the product that I found myself as a consultant. I saw the pink Cadillac and set my mind to winning it. I won it in 1981. I made Directorship in eleven months. My picture was placed in the Chicago Defender Newspaper, telling my story. When Mary Kay called me and rewarded me with the Pink Cadillac car, I was so out of it. I asked God for it and He gave me the knowhow to get it: work, work, work, hard work. Nothing is given to you; you have to earn your way. You then can really praise and give God the glory for giving you the strength to succeed. I got to meet her personally and visited her home in Texas. We Directors in training got to take pictures with her. What a nice Lady and boss Lady she was. We do miss that beautiful face, smile, and sweet voice. I was so up on cloud nine when they brought me the Pink Cadillac, I forgot to take pictures. But that's okay. They got to see me drive it with my name on it. God is good all the time. Great things He has done for me.

I never thought that I would be recognized by the Biltmore Who's Who as an Exclusive Lifetime Honored Member, but I was, with a press release. That was surprising and exciting. Another surprise was to be recognized by the Metro Area Professional Organization (MAPO), at an Honors Dinner. It was a grand night, thanks to Dr. John Q. Owens and his wife, Dr. Dorothy Owens, Co-Founders. People I never knew or even thought of as recognizing me knew me and blessed my soul. There is a God that watches over me and gives His "Miracle Baby" favor.

The many good jobs I've had required a college degree, but because of my good record, dependability, and excellent people skills, I was hired. I was promoted all the way up to Executive Regional Trainer at Carson, Pirie, Scott in Chicago, Ill. Nobody but the Lord can give you that kind of favor. He said in His Word, Psalms 37:4, that if I delight myself in Him (the Lord), He will give me the desires of my heart. I believe, and I receive, thank you Jesus. I always wanted to go back to school and get a Degree. He blessed me to do so in 2006-2010, at the Metropolitan Christian Bible Institute/Advantage College where I received my Associates and Bachelor Degrees. That was a day to celebrate my God's love for me. He was my strong tower that gave me the strength to reach the finish line, march across that stage and receive my diplomas. I earned a 4.0 on my Official Transcript, that's a beautiful sight. To God be the Glory.

My Beautiful Parents the late Rev. Damon Jones Sr. and Missionary Willie Ann Jones, the greatest parents that ever lived; I give God the Praise and the Honor for showering us with the blessing of having our Mother and Father as long as we did. I can only speak for myself, and I know I will see them again in Glory. My prayer is that we all will be together in Glory, praising His Mighty, Wondrous name.

"Miracle Baby" Anointed By God In My Mother's Womb, signing off until next time …

Mary Kay Pictures

CHICAGO DEFENDER - WEDNESDAY, AUGUST 13, 1981 15

Jean Johnson has completed her training as a Director-in-Qualification and is now a Professional Sales Director with Mary Kay Cosmetics, Inc. She became a director within eleven months of being in the company. Recently she spent a week attending a Leadership Conference consisting of Directors only and Jamboree, where over 6,000 women and men attended. Chairman of the Board, Mary Kay Ash, and staff conducted inspirational and _____ Jamboree with a theme of "Capture The Vision."

State Queens

August

Illinois—Director Jean Johnson

Minnesota—Stephany Thurnau, S. Reiter
   Unit

North Dakota—Director Punky Savageau

South Dakota—Helen Hendry, K.
   Kratochvil Unit

Wisconsin—Joyce Wolfe, C. Strang Unit

Who's Who Pictures

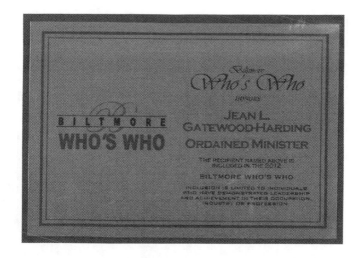

Biltmore Who's Who

RECOGNIZES

Jean L. Gatewood-Harding

Ordained Minister

AS AN

EXCLUSIVE LIFETIME HONORED MEMBER

THE ABOVE NAMED INDIVIDUAL HAS QUALIFIED

FOR INCLUSION IN THE 2012 EDITION OF THE

BILTMORE WHO'S WHO REGISTRY

OF EXECUTIVES AND PROFESSIONALS

In Witness Whereof
this Award is issued and signed by _____

Chairman

January 23, 2012

Date of Admission

"What do you do"

"When God puts you on hold"

Matthew 15:21--28

21. Then Jesus went thence, and departed into the coasts of Tyre and Sidon.
22. And behold a woman of Canaan came out of the same coasts,and cried unto Him saying,Have mercy on me O Lord, thou Son of David; my daughter is grievously vexed with a devil.
23. But He answered her not a word. And His disciples came and besought Him, saying, Send her away; for she crieth after us.
24. But He answered and said, I am not sent but unto the lost sheep of the house of Israel.

25. Then she came and worshipped Him, saying, Lord, help me.

26. But He answered and said, it is not meet to take the children's bread, and to cast it to dogs.

27. And she said, Truth, Lord: yet the dogs eat of the crumbs which falls from their Masters' table.

28. Then Jesus answered and said unto her, O woman, great is thy faith: be it unto thee even as thou wilt. And her daughter was made whole from that very hour.

We live in the day of fast forward, microwave dinners, wrinkle free clothes, already cooked bacon, sausage,etc.. No time to look up a number, just call the operator. We're to busy to enjoy life. But every now and then, we're put on hold weather we like it or not. We get stuck in traffic, but oh, that's okay, I can just use my cell and take care of business or let them know where I am. How about this, have a very important phone call to make, and you get the answering machine. It comes on and ask you questions you don't have time for but you have to take the time because you are stuck! The system tells you, if you want to speak to john press 1, Jean, press 2, if you have a complaint, press 3. After pressing all those numbers, you get another recording which says, your waiting time is 10 minutes, When you're finally through with all of the run around, the system says, I'm not able to take your call, please leave your name, your number, and a short message, and I will return your call just as soon as possible. We are not a society that wait with ease. Our patience is shallow and our temper very short. We're spoiled to fax machines, over night delivery, 10 minutes without electricity sends us up a wall. You have a sick child, or mother, or you or someone in the family is sick or in trouble. You've been praying and seeking God to heal or fix a situation and it seem as thou God is no where around, He's just not hearing you. What do you do. Take things in your own hands and mess up just as Sarah did when she gave Abraham Haggai her handmaiden. Or how about Abraham when he lied twice about Sarah being his sister, when she really was his wife. He almost caused Abimelech to sin which could have caused his life. God move in His own time. We say He may not come when you want Him, but He's right on time, do we believe it? We, like Abraham and Sarah take thing in our own hand and mess up big time, and then we really want to blame God, but we know that's not true. Take a good look at the Canaanite woman, and her faith in the God we say we have faith in. He will truly never leave us nor forsake us. What would you do if God put you on hold. 1. You keep trusting him, 2, Hold fast to God's unchanging hand, and number 3, Don;t give up, don't give in, don't give out. Help is on the way. Hebrew 13:5-6 and Joshua 1:5.

"MIRACLE BABY", Anointed By God In My
Mother's Womb. To God Be The Glory.

Printed in the United States
By Bookmasters